Accelerate to Awesome!

How to Get Clarity, Remove Distractions, and Achieve Your Goals Now

**By
Etrulia Troy Lee M.Ed., Ph.D.
Empress of Empowerment**

Copyright©2016 by Etrulia Reid Lee, M.Ed., Ph.D.

Publisher: Women Enlightened & Economically Empowered, LLC Fort Washington, Maryland

All rights reserved. No part of this book may be reproduced in any form by any electronic or mechanical means, including information and retrieval systems, without permission in writing from the publisher, except by a reviewer, who may quote brief passages in a review.

Printed in the United States of America

Disclaimer:

This publication is for informational purposes only. It is neither the intent of the author or the publisher to render professional services to the reader. It is not intended to diagnose, treat, cure, or prevent any mental or physical health problem. It is not intended to be a substitute for medical or psychological help. The author and publisher specifically disclaim all responsibility for any liability, loss, injury, or risk, personal or otherwise, which is incurred as a result of or consequence, directly or indirectly, from the use or application of any contents in the book.

Scripture references, unless other indicated are taken from New King James Version®. Copyright © 1982 by Thomas Nelson, Inc. Used by permission. All rights reserved.

Scripture taken from the HOLY BIBLE, NEW INTERNATIONAL VERSION®. Copyright © 1973, 1978, 1984 Biblica. Used by permission of Zondervan. All rights reserved. The "NIV" and "New
International Version" trademarks are registered in the United States Patent and Trademark Office by Biblica. Use of either trademark requires the permission of Biblica.

Any and all product names referred to in this publication are the trademarks and property of their respective owners. None of these owners has sponsored, authorized, endorsed or approved this publication in any way. The author received no financial remuneration for mentioning any products in this publication.

ISBN 978-0-9982624-0-6

DEDICATION

I dedicate this book to my mother, Etrulia Lucille Chapel Reid, who earned her angel wings on August 17, 2016, and now safely resides in heaven. God blessed my mother with ninety years of life on this earth and I am eternally grateful for the life that my mother lived. I count it one of life's biggest blessings that I, being her 7th child and 4th daughter, was honored to be named after her.

Mommy's life was not an easy one. She was separated for many years from her mother as a child and lived with her father and stepmother who were less than nurturing. She survived a gunshot wound at age three. She raised nine children without the support of a dependable husband. She was mainly the sole support for the family, working many long hours as a seamstress at Caldwell Dress Factory. Although she was stricken with multiple sclerosis for over 30 years and lost her ability to ambulate independently when she was seventy, she was never stricken in her spirit.

Mommy was tenacious, sassy, funny, and had an indomitable fighter spirit. She was full of wisdom in her golden years even as it was intermingled with some dementia and delusional thinking. I admire my mother for many reasons, but one quality in particular that I want to honor her for is gratitude. Despite the toll that multiple sclerosis took on her body and the fact that she lived in a nursing home for the last fifteen years of her life, she was not a complainer. She chose to look at the blessings she did have rather than what she did not have in terms of physical health. What she lacked in possessions, she imagined she did have them and she was the grand queen. She loved her family and she was proud of our accomplishments.

She taught me many lessons about always doing the best with what you have. She taught me how to fall down and get back up. Thank you, Mommy! aka, Trudy, Tru-Tru, Tru-ster, Tru-fi-Trudy!

FOREWORD

How Firm a Foundation!

It will become very apparent to anyone reading this book very quickly that I am a believer in God the Father, God the Son, and God the Holy Spirit. I am grateful that I was raised in the church and fully embraced the Christian walk at age 29. Christians are referred to as being saved, born again, and/or believers. It is all the same and the foundation is accepting the truth of the death, burial, and resurrection of Jesus and what that means regarding your life on the earth and your life in eternity.

If you have never accepted Jesus Christ as your Lord and savior, I urge you to consider what it means to be saved and all the benefits, both in the present and in eternity, that salvation offers. Being saved is as simple as 1, 2, 3. You don't need to be in church to get saved or need a preacher to usher you into salvation. You just need to believe and embrace the truth. And here is the truth from the word of God. All the following scriptures are taken from the New King James Version of the Bible.

Romans 3:23: *"For all have sinned and fall short of the glory of God."* All means all and that means you and me.

Romans 3:10: *"As it is written: "There is none righteous, no, not one."* I am not righteous; you are not righteous. Only God is.

Romans 5:12: *"Therefore, just as through one man sin entered the world, and death through sin, and thus death spread to all men, because all have sinned."* The original sin that entered the world was through Adam. The story of Adam can be found in Genesis 2:4-3:24.

Romans 6:23: *"For the wages of sin is death, but the gift of God is eternal life in Christ Jesus our Lord."* If you die without accepting the gift of eternal life through belief in Christ, you will spend eternity in a state of death separated from God. This is known as hell.

Romans 5:8: *"But God demonstrates His own love toward us, in that while we were still sinners, Christ died for us."* Christ paid our sin debt. This was God's plan since the beginning of the world for Christ to reconcile us to God.

Romans 10:9-10: *That if you confess with your mouth the Lord Jesus and believe in your heart that God has raised Him from the dead, you will be saved. For with the heart one believes unto righteousness, and with the mouth confession is made unto salvation."* This is what is required to be saved, born again, become a Christian, be a child of God. You must confess and believe.

Romans 10:13: *"For whoever calls on the name of the Lord shall be saved."*

If you have never done so, I encourage you to call on the name of the Lord right where you are right now. This simple prayer of faith is all you need.

The prayer below is taken from http://salvationprayer.info/home/salvation/. There is nothing official about this prayer and it is not found anywhere in the Bible. It embodies the concepts that were taught by Jesus and articulated in the scriptures that you just read above. The entire prayer is not copied; just the essentials of what a prayer to accept Jesus as your Lord and savior and become saved should contain.

"Dear God in heaven, I come to you in the name of Jesus. I acknowledge to You that I am a sinner, and I am sorry for my sins and the life that I have lived; I need your forgiveness. I believe that your only begotten Son Jesus Christ shed His precious blood on the cross at Calvary and died for my sins, and I am now willing to turn from my sin. You said in Your Holy Word, Romans 10:9 that if we confess the Lord our God and believe in our hearts that God raised Jesus from the dead, we shall be saved. Right now, I confess Jesus as the Lord of my soul. With my heart, I believe that God raised Jesus from the dead. This very moment I accept Jesus Christ as my own personal Savior and according to His Word, right now I am saved. Thank you, Jesus, for your unlimited grace which has saved me from my sins."

If you just prayed that prayer for the first time, the angels in heaven are rejoicing!

Luke 15:7: *"Just so, I tell you, there will be more joy in heaven over one sinner who repents than over ninety-nine righteous persons who need not repentance."*

I would be honored to know if you accepted Christ because of what you just read and I would love to send you a free gift to help you grow as a Christian. Please send me an email at info@womeneee.com and share your story.

Table Of Contents

Is There A "But" In Your Way? 9

What do You Really Want? 15

Understanding Fear 27

Moving Past Your Fears 45

Aligning Your Goals With the True You 63

What Motivates You? 75

Your Action Plan 79

Affirmations 95

Vision Boards 105

Get Around The Right People 111

Time To Accelerate!!! 117

About The Author 119

Chapter One

Is There A "But" In Your Way?

- I would lose weight but….
- I would go back to school but….
- I would change jobs but….
- I would exercise but….
- I would apply for the promotion at work but….
- I would drink more water but….
- I would save more money but….
- I would set goals but….
- I would stop eating out but….
- I would treat my spouse better but….
- I would invest spend more time with my spouse but….
- I would watch less T.V. but….
- I would spend more time with my kids but…
- I would write the book I have been meaning to write but….
- I would visit my parents more but….
- I would drink less coffee but….
- I would read more but….
- I would keep my home cleaner but….
- I would forgive him but….
- I would give more to charity but….
- I would be in a ministry at church but….

- I would stop smoking but….
- I would stop drinking but
- I would slow down and drive slower but….
- I would get healthier but….
- I would move to another city but….
- I would stop using my credit cards but….
- I would get out of debt but….
- I would….
- I would….
- I would….

> *"He that is good at making excuses is seldom good for anything else."* Benjamin Franklin

But…… that is one little word that has a big impact on the lives of so many people. It keeps dreams from being realized, potential from being achieved, degrees from being earned, relationships from being healed, health from being restored, and it keeps you from accelerating to the awesome life that you want!

So, what are your buts? Did you identify with any in the list? How much impact are your buts having on your life? Is your but worth what you are missing out on?

You cannot accelerate to awesome until you deal with your buts. At the root of all buts is one of two causes. First, buts are an excuse for not doing something that you don't want to do anyway. You may not really want to stop smoking, but your spouse is nagging you to do it. You may not really want the promotion at work because of the added responsibility and headache, but you feel you should want it. You really don't want to lose the weight but since everyone is talking about weight loss, you might as well talk about it too.

Many people are living a life that they did not design for themselves. They have kind of gone along with the flow and have found themselves where they are today. They are living somebody else's idea of what their life should be like. It could be what their parents wanted them to do, what they thought was safe, or where the jobs were plentiful. They go to work every day disconnected from their true self.

This is a major cause of unhappiness. Have you asked someone, *"How did you get in this line of work?"* and they answered, *"I just kind of fell into it."* You do know that falling is an accident, right?

So, it is no surprise that people find a lot of excuses for not doing certain things because, the truth is, they really don't want to do it.

The second root of all buts is fear. Fear comes in many forms:
- Fear of failure

- Fear of being inadequate
- Fear of being ridiculed
- Fear of going against the grain
- Fear of the unknown
- Fear of change
- Fear of rejection
- Fear of success
- Fear of being embarrassed
- Fear of not being supported
- Fear of losing it all
- Fear of being vulnerable
- Fear of not making enough money
- Fear of missing out on something

The people who fall into this category have a dream and a life that they want, but they are just too afraid to go for it. This is about to end for you!

> "The heart has its reasons but the mind makes the excuses." Amit Abraham

So, which category do you fall into? If you are not sure, I am going to help you to determine that. It could be that some of your buts are excuses for things you really don't want to do and others are because of fears. Either way, getting to the root cause of your buts will free you to either stop saying that you want to do something or help free you from your fears so you can accelerate to create the life you want.

Chapter Two
What do You Really Want?

Assignment One

Make a list of all the things that you think you want but have either not pursued or are stalled in pursing. Include the reason why you think you have not moved forward. This is a time to be very honest with yourself. Do not rush through this. Address the major areas of your life, including personal relationships, health, weight, career, where you live, hobbies, finances, vacations, etc.

I want to:

_____
_____
_____
_____

I have not done this because:

_____
_____
_____
_____

I want to:

_____
_____
_____
_____

I have not done this because:

_____
_____
_____
_____

I want to:

_____
_____
_____
_____

I have not done this because:

_____
_____
_____
_____

I want to:

_____
_____
_____
_____

I have not done this because:

_____
_____
_____
_____

I want to:

_____
_____
_____
_____

I have not done this because:

_____
_____
_____
_____

I want to:
_____
_____
_____
_____
_____

I have not done this because:
_____
_____
_____
_____
_____

I want to:
_____
_____
_____
_____
_____

I have not done this because:
_____
_____
_____
_____
_____

> *"How pitiful is an intelligence used only to make excuses to quieten the conscience."* <u>Ignazio Silone</u>

Assignment Two

You are going to answer four very important questions that will help determine what you really want out of life. Without pondering these questions, write what immediately pops in your mind. Ready? Let's do it!

What would you do if you knew you could not fail?

_____
_____
_____
_____
_____
_____
_____
_____

What would you do for free?

_____
_____
_____
_____

_____
_____
_____
_____

If money was no object, how would you choose to live your life?
_____
_____
_____
_____
_____
_____
_____
_____

What is it that you enjoy doing and that people compliment you on?
_____
_____
_____
_____
_____
_____
_____
_____

Hold on to these answers because we will come back to them.

> *"We may place blame, give reasons, and even have excuses; but in the end, it is an act of cowardice to not follow your dreams."* Steve Maraboli

Assignment Three

Look at the list of the things that you want to do but have not done yet or are stalled in doing. Rate each thing you wrote from 1-10, with one being that it is not that important and ten being that this is something you really want to do.

Now look at your list carefully. Look at the ones that you scored 5 or below. Is this your goal or is it somebody else's goal? Is it something that you have believed that you should do, or do you really want to do it?

A lot of things that we think we should do are because we are comparing ourselves with others. I love the expression credited to the Iyanla Vanzant, *"Comparison is an act of violence against the self."* If you are comparing yourself with others, you will always find someone who is richer, smarter, prettier, wittier, better liked, etc. Part of you being able to accelerate to awesome is to relieve the burden of you feeling you are not measuring up because you are comparing yourself to others. You are already awesome … now you are going to accelerate it to a higher level!

Comparing ourselves to others begins early in the socialization process – as young as preschool. When you were in preschool and someone got three cookies on their plate for their snack and you only got two, there was going to be trouble. The fact that you only got two cookies made you "less than" the other person.

As we continue in school we learn that the A student is more prized and valued than the C student. For the A student, the pressure is there to keep the A; for the C student they feel less worthy than the A student. This act of comparison begins to chip away at our self-esteem.

As we grow, we see other examples of achievement held in high esteem, whether it be a person's looks, athleticism, academic achievement, or material possessions. We are caught in a cycle of comparison that can be crushing to our overall happiness. We begin to believe that we should do more and be more.

For those things that we don't yet possess or those qualities that we have not quite cultivated, but believe that we should have/be, we begin to make excuses.

Rather than making excuses, we must examine if this was a path that we were meant to be on in the first place.

Your Creator made you unique. Of all the billions of people who are on the face of the earth now, and of all the billions of people who have lived and died, there has never been anyone like you. Part of living a life that is awesome is to make sure that these issues that you have been making excuses for are part of who you are supposed to be.

> *"To be yourself in a world that is constantly trying to make you something else is the greatest accomplishment."* Ralph Waldo Emerson

I will never forget the day a friend of my mine called me and this is what she said:

"I am calling to let you know that I really admire you. I was just sitting here thinking about how you just moved into your house and you have all your window coverings up and I have been in my house for several years and still don't some of my windows done. I was also thinking about all the new initiatives you have created at church on the Social Committee. Before you joined our church, our anniversary celebration was apple juice and cookies, and now we are celebrating at

Martin's Crosswinds. You have so much energy and just know how to get things done. I used to look at you and feel bad because I was not like you. Then I realized I would never be like you and that was O.K. I am O.K. with who I am. But I wanted you to know that I really appreciate you."

You could have knocked me over with a feather! I share this story not to pat myself on the back or to be boastful. I used to always say of this woman that she probably had the lowest of low blood pressure and would live to be 100 years old! Nothing ever seemed to rattle her and she always appeared to be on chill mode. So while she was admiring me, I was looking at her thinking I needed to cool out! This is an example of a woman with excellent self-esteem. She was comfortable with who she was but could appreciate the talent of others.

Notice she said that she used to feel bad when she was comparing what I had done to what she had done. But once she accepted the fact that she was not me and she was who she was, she was O.K. with it. She could stop looking at her windows and making excuses for them not being done. She then benefitted from peace of mind. Having peace of mind is an awesome state to be in! She in a very real way created a better life for herself by letting it go.

As we go through the remainder of this book, don't think you are going to get a magic formula for doing things that go against who you are as a person. My goal is to get you in touch with what you really want versus what you have been saying that you want. And once we discover what you really want, we can an awesome action plan to accelerate your progress to get there.

So getting back to things on your list that you scored 5 or less. Do you really want to do those things? If so, great, then we are going to help you tackle them. If not, just let them go!

If you are ready to move some of the items off your list, look at that item and say, *"I am removing this as clutter from my mind. I will no longer make an excuse for not doing this. This is not a priority for my life and I am O.K. with that. I am a good person and this does not define me. It may be O.K. for somebody else, but this is not for me. I release it."* And as a believer in Jesus Christ, I always end with, *"In Jesus' name, Amen!"*

> *"The worst loneliness is to not be comfortable with yourself."* Mark Twain

Chapter Three
Understanding Fear

Assignment Four

Look back over the items in Chapter Two that you ranked above five. Ask yourself the same questions. Is this your goal or is it somebody else's goal? Is it something that you have made yourself feel guilty about, believing that you should do it, or do you really want to do it?

There is an expression that says, *"Where there is a will there is a way."* People find a way to do the things they really want to do. However, this does not negate the fact that, when attempting something new, fear can come in and halt you in your tracks.

There are many acronyms for fear.
- False Expectations Appearing Real.
- Future Events Appearing Real.
- Future Events Already Ruined.
- Failure Expected And Received.
- Finding Everything A Roadblock.

My favorite acronym when it comes to not moving forward with something that you want to do is Finding Excuses And Reasons.

When we are fearful, it is because we are projecting a negative outcome about a future event. Our projection is loaded with 'what ifs?' and all of the ifs predict disaster. We have experienced more made-up drama and trauma in our heads than we have experienced in real life. When you create fear in your mind, it has no boundaries. It is free to run amok and spin the most horrific circumstances.

Stop for a moment and think about all the times that you were fearful. You may have been fearful about the outcome of a medical test, fearful that you had not heard from someone and wondered if everything was O.K., fearful about the fact that you heard your company was laying off workers, etc. Think of how you stressed and worried, only to have a positive outcome. How many times were our worst fears not realized?

> *"I learned that courage was not the absence of fear, but the triumph over it. The brave man is not he who does not feel afraid, but he who conquers that fear."* Nelson Mandela

I recall when my youngest son was deployed to Iraq in 2005. Never in a million years had I thought that I would be the mother of son fighting a war in a foreign country. I was raised during the Vietnam era and was all too familiar with grieving families who lost their father/son/brother/husband/cousin in the war. That was not an experience that I wanted on my plate.

When Michael left the barracks in Maryland in June 2005 on the first leg of his journey to Iraq, I was shaken, but comforted by the fact that he was going to Indiana for training first. I was given false hope that we could travel to Indiana in 8 weeks to see him off before he went to Iraq. This turned out not to be true. We spoke with him right before his unit pulled out in August.

This is when a deep fear seized me. No, it paralyzed me. No, it terrorized me! The thought that he would be harm's way and that I may never see him alive again took over my thoughts. I did everything I knew to do to chase away my fears. I prayed, I quoted scripture, I sang happy songs, but nothing shook it. I was physically ill for several days after he left and could not function.

But God! Knowing that he gifted me with the ability to write, he gave me this poem in one sitting. It flowed out of me and was the only thing that kept my mind at peace during his tenure in Iraq. I titled the poem *Fear*.

What is fear, but your imagination running wild?
Like being afraid of the dark when you were a child.
A thought takes hold and becomes larger than life,

Causing you turmoil, anguish and undue strife.
You dwell on it, you can't shake it loose,
It possesses you, you cannot call a truce.
Forgetting that the fear only exists in your mind,
You project it into the future, which you know will be unkind.
The outcome is grim, you know you are in for a rough ride,
The tears come unabated, just like a rising tide.
Day turns to night and night back into day,
And your fear greets you each morning, it never goes away.
You have all but surrendered to your prophecy of doom,
Knowing it is inevitable, you live in your gloom.
But if your thoughts are the only thing you really own,
Then why have you allowed this fear to become full blown?
Your reality is what you dwell on, it is real for you.
Why not see brighter tomorrows and skies of blue?
Knowing that there are many things not in your control
But your thoughts you can navigate and let peace take hold.
You control your own mind and can choose good thoughts or bad.
Let this truth resonate in your spirit, and you'll only have time to be glad.

For God says he has not given us a spirit of fear, Keep this thought in your mind, and know that He is near. Copyrighted©2005

Michael returned safely from Iraq in August of 2006. He has since been deployed twice, back to Iraq and in Afghanistan. Each time he left, I pulled out this poem and read it until I calmed down. Michael now lives about five minutes away from my home with his wife and son. All praises to God!

> "Do not anticipate trouble, or worry about what may never happen. Keep in the sunlight." Benjamin

At the root of all fear is the fear of loss.

- You are fearful of a bad report from the doctor because you could lose your life or your health.
- You are fearful of public speaking because people may ridicule your speaking and you might lose the respect of others.
- You are fearful when your loved doesn't arrive home at the expected time because he/she may not be O.K. and you could lose him/her.
- You are fearful of job loss because you could lose your standard of living.

- You are fearful of new social situations because people may not accept you and you would lose your sense of self-worth.
- You are fearful of disciplining your children because you could lose their love.
- You are fearful of speaking up when you see others doing the wrong thing because you don't want to lose the feeling of being comfortable.

When it comes to stepping out of our comfort zone to pursue a goal, the number one thing that holds us back is fear of failure. With failure could come the loss of time, money, respect of others, social status, etc.

Tied to a fear of failure is a lack of self-confidence/lack of self-esteem. If you are always thinking you are going to fail, then you may need to examine the root cause of this. There are many reasons why people lack self-confidence. Among them are:

- Disapproving parents/caregivers
- Indifferent parents/caregivers
- Parental conflict in the home
- Dysfunctional families
- Bullying by siblings
- Bullying by others
- Overprotective parents
- Academic challenges

- Physical disabilities
- Childhood abuse
- Childhood sexual abuse
- Religious belief systems
- Poverty

If you feel that you lack basic self-confidence, and you identified with one or more of the above situations, then I highly recommend that you seek additional resources to heal you from your past. It is beyond the scope of this book to address self-esteem issues.

I suffered from low-esteem for many, many years. There were three things that I identified as being at the root of my low self-esteem.

- Disapproving parent: I love my mamma, but my daddy drama – that could fill a book!
- Sibling bullying: This came in the form of being told constantly that I had no common sense. I was also nicknamed "Spook" because I apparently widened my eyes a lot when I talked (still do) and was fearful a lot of the time. Being the 7th of 9 children, it is often hard to live up to older siblings' expectations.
- Poverty: We were by far the poorest family on the block.

Of all the moments that shaped the healthy self-esteem that I have today, two stand out as turning points.

The first one happened when I was married for about a year. I was extremely jealous when it came to my husband spending time with or talking to anyone other than me. At the root of this was insecurity because I felt I had "married up." I also was raised on a steady diet of "all men are dogs," "men need more than one hole to run to," "men are no good," etc., etc., etc. You know the drill. So an inner-city girl like me marrying a man who grew up in the first black suburb of the D.C. Metro area, who lived in a single-family home (I only knew people who had row houses), both of his parents were college educated (we were the first generation in our family to go to college), he spoke the king's English, and seemed like an all-around genuine nice guy – I knew this was too good to be true.

I remember just waiting for something to go wrong that first year of marriage. If we were out at an event and he spoke to another female, I was sure he was trying to get her phone number to cheat on me. Or if his best buddy came in town and they went out together, it was only because they were on the hunt (never mind that his best buddy was married too). I had fits of rage if he was late coming home from work (he must have stopped by on the way home to see some chick). You talk about a hot mess!

One day my husband came home and asked me to dial a number. I responded, "Who am I calling?"

He said, "Just dial the number please." I did. I had dialed into the Prince George's County Library system audio file. He then told me to put in a series of numbers that corresponded to the tape that he wanted me to listen to. I complied. The recorder then said, "This is tape 5609, Jealousy and its Root Causes."

I was boiling mad! How dare he accuse me of being jealous! At that moment I wanted to throw the phone at him, but instead I gave him my meanest glare and kept the phone in hand and continued to listen. I always say that was only God!

As I listened to the recording, it was like someone had been following me around. They could have easily inserted my name right in the tape. I so strongly identified with what they were saying that it took me aback. When the tape concluded, I said not a word to my husband but went straight upstairs to be alone.

My emotions were all over the place. I was furious that he thought I was jealous and had the nerve to have me listen to the tape. I was alarmed that the tape described me to a T. I was ashamed that I was the way the tape described. I was feeling pitiful and couldn't believe I had to face up to what we both now knew. And I was contemplative because I knew that I did not want to be that person.

It took me about an hour before I came downstairs and said to my husband, "I don't want to keep behaving this way. I want to change. I'm sorry for my bad behavior in the past, and I am going to do better."

And as we all know, easier said than done. I no longer acted out on my thoughts, but they still came. The self-control I had to exercise to not act on my thoughts was tantamount to trying to hold back the water in the Hoover Dam! Each time I would take deep breaths, put a smile on face, and talk myself down off the ledge. But the more I did it, the easier it became. I had to go through the process.

Now when you take a closer look at this, my actions were being driven by fear. Fear that I was not good enough for him and fear that I would lose him. I got rid of the fear by facing the truth, creating an action plan, and going through with it.

> *"Low self-esteem is like driving through life with your hand-brake on."* Maxwell Maltz

I had my second major moment of clarity was when I found out I was smart at 26 years old. Up until this time, I was waiting to be uncovered as the stupid person I really was. Constantly hearing that I had no common sense had taken root in what I believed about myself.

I graduated from high school with 5 As, 1 B, and 1 C. That one C came from a history teacher who (for real, for real) did not like me. I was rather militant in the early 70s, considered myself an East Coast Black Panther, and loved quoting Gil Scott Heron (the revolution will not be televised!). This teacher so did not like me that when I showed him my acceptance letter to Carnegie Mellon University with a full scholarship, he had the temerity to say to me, "That letter is not yours. You made it up." And he was serious! Now let me remind you of the technology we had back then – I could have no more made that letter up than I could have grown green horns!

Back to my narrative. When I looked at the good grades I got in high school, I explained them away by saying, "Well, it was an inner-city school and the standards were not that high."

I graduated from Cabrini College with a 3.49 GPA. I explained that away by saying it was a small Catholic school.

I enrolled in a graduate program at the University of Maryland, College Park, to study for Masters in education. Part of my program was graduate level statistics. When the semester started, there were about 140 students in the class. By the time the semester was over, it had dwindled to about 70. It was a tough class, but I hung in there.

Back then, the final grades were posted outside of the classroom by your student I.D. When I went to check my final grade, I was shocked to see an 'A' by my name. The first thing I did was look up and down the hall in a panic. Don't ask me why I did this. In hindsight, I think it was because I thought somebody surely was going to come running down the hall screaming that the grade was not mine. I looked at the grade again, and double-checked to make sure it was mine, and yep! There it stood with my number beside it. My mind then said, "Everybody must have gotten an A." So, I checked everyone else's grade. Only two other A's where there. At that moment, I said to myself, "This is a major university. The students in the class were overwhelmingly white. Half of the class dropped out. Only three people got an A I was one of them. I must not be stupid."

Notice I did not tell myself that I was smart, just that I wasn't stupid. Pitiful, right?

This is how I broke the news to my husband about my grade when I got home. "Guess what? I'm not stupid. I got an A in statistics and only 3 people in the entire class got an A and I was one of them. I really am not stupid!"

Of course, he looked at me like I was stupid! I can't remember his exact response, but it was along the lines of him saying that he always thought I was super smart, and he could not believe that I ever thought anything else.

I remember just glowing over the next several days in wonderment that I really was smart. From that moment on, I found myself relaxing more in all kinds of social environments, even at work. I had a newfound confidence that I was smart and no longer had to worry about being found out.

When you look at this scenario, at the root of my issue was fear. Fear that I was not good enough. Fear that I could not measure up. Fear that I would be found out. Thank God that he orchestrated these circumstances to bring me out of my shell so I could unapologetically embrace who I was really was.

> *"With realization of one's own potential and self-confidence in one's ability, one can build a better world."* Dalai Lama

Many people have good self-confidence and high self-esteem, but they still may be reluctant to go after something they want because of fear of failure. Our reptilian brain is always trying to keep us safe. Where you are right now is safe. Trying something new will put you outside of your comfort zone. Why take the risk?

Here is why: Studies show that among the top things that people regret right before they die is not facing their fears and going for something that they really wanted to do.

> *"Fear will pass, but regrets will last forever."* Author Unknown

An article in *Inc. Magazine* (http://www.inc.com/lolly-daskal/12-things-people-regret-the-most-before-they-die.html) noted that the 12 things people regret at the end of life are as follows:

- They wish they had spent more time with the people they loved.
- They wish they had worried less.
- They wish they had forgiven more.
- They wish they had stood up for themselves.
- They wish they had lived their own life.
- They wish they had been more honest, i.e., owning up to their own elemental truth.
- They wish they had worked less.
- They wish they had cared less about what other people think.
- They wish they had lived up to their full potential.
- They wish they had faced their fears. Fear is only temporary, but regret lasts forever.
- They wish they had stopped chasing the wrong things
- They wish they had lived more in the moment.

> "Should ofs and could ofs are words we don't use; they only depress us and give us the blues." Carol Burnett

Assignment Five

Right now, right at this moment, I want you to stop reading this book and spend a few minutes contemplating what you just read. How does it make you feel? Do you feel you want to spring into action? Did you feel a feeling of regret creeping over you? Did you hear yourself say, "I know, but…"? I urge you to sit with your feelings for just a moment. Then, I want you to write down what came to mind as you reflected on what you read.

My Reflection

_____
_____
_____
_____
_____
_____
_____
_____
_____
_____
_____
_____
_____
_____
_____
_____

Chapter Four
Moving Past Your Fears

Assignment Six

So now you have the things on your list that you scored above 5 and maybe some that scored below 5. I want you to rank these items from 1 to 3. This time 1 will be the goal that you really want to achieve. If you rank more than one thing a 1, that is O.K.

Now write only the things here that you ranked number 1. Create a new sheet for each number 1 item that you came up with.

I want to

_____
_____
_____

This is important to me because

_____
_____
_____
_____

I first became aware that I wanted to do (how many years/months ago; what were the circumstances?)

_____
_____
_____
_____
_____

The ways my life will be different when I achieve this goal are

_____
_____
_____
_____
_____

If I don't achieve this goal, I think I will feel

_____
_____
_____
_____

The reason I have not pursued this is because

_____
_____
_____

_____

_____

_____

The best possible outcome if I move forward and pursue this is

_____

_____

_____

_____

_____

The worst possible outcome is

_____

_____

_____

_____

_____

If the worst happens, what happens next?

_____

_____

_____

_____

_____

Then what would happen after that?
_____
_____
_____
_____
_____

Then what would happen after that?
_____
_____
_____
_____
_____

Then what would happen after that?
_____
_____
_____
_____
_____

Then what would happen after that?
_____
_____
_____
_____
_____

_____

_____

Keep going with this until you reach the last possible thing that could happen if you moved forward and went for your goal and it did not work out as intended. If it doesn't end in death (most of us do want to live), ask yourself this last question:

If this were the outcome, could I live with that? _____.

If the answer is yes, move forward. If the answer is no, you have two options.

Option A: Stop stressing about what you think you want to do. You really don't want to do it. You are much more comfortable where you are. AND THIS IS O.K. There is a lot of freedom in knowing that you are satisfied with yourself. This is part of creating your best life.

Option B: Examine what fear may be holding you back.

> *"Choices made, whether bad or good, follow you forever and affect everyone in their path one way or another." J.E.B. Spredemann*

The method used above of looking at a situation and figuring out the worst-case scenario, and then stepping back and asking yourself if you could live with that outcome is useful in all kinds of situations. I use this formula often with my clients, both for life coaching and weight loss.

Let me give you two examples of how I used the above formula, once with a friend and once when I used it for myself.

I was speaking with one of my daughter-friends on the phone. This was in the age when phone companies were charging for long-distance. Her husband was in the navy, deployed overseas, and she was pregnant with their third child. She was away from her family and ran up a rather sizeable long-distance bill between talking to her husband and her family.

She was in a panicked and fearful state when she saw the phone bill of $600. She was expressing how awful it was going to be to tell her husband about this bill. She was crying and wringing her hands. I asked her the following:

Me: What is going to happen when you tell John (not his real name) about the bill?

Her: He is going to blow his top! (sniffle) He is always saying that I am not responsible with money and this is going to make him mad. (sniffle, sniffle, sniffle) I can just hear him going off now. It is going to be really bad. (crying)

Me: Then what is going to happen?

Her: What do you mean?

Me: What is going to happen after he blows his top and fusses at you?

Her: He is going to be mad for a while. He will probably restrict my access to the accounts, tell me to stay off the phone, try and cut my budget in other areas, you know, stuff like that.

Me: Then what is going to happen?

Her: Oh, I don't know. He'll probably not call me for a week or two to let me know he is mad.

Me: Then what is going to happen?

Her: I guess he'll eventually get over it. He is going to have to.

Me: So in the end, nobody dies, nobody gets hurt, no divorce, and life goes on.

Her: Yeah, I guess that is about right.

She then started to laugh. Not a belly laugh and not a nervous laugh, but a laugh of relief. She had faced her worst fears, taken it out to the final conclusion, and decided it wasn't so bad after all!

> *"Nothing in life is to be feared. It is only to be understood."* Marie Curie

My husband and I used the above formula when I was contemplating quitting my good-paying job with my lofty title. I had a plan and a strategy but, as we all know, the best laid plans of mice of men are subject to go astray. This was the process.

Us: What is the worst that could happen if I leave this position?

Answer: You will be leaving the security of direct deposit and you may not make the money you are projecting you are going to make on your own.

Us: What might happen after that?

Answer: We may not make as much money as the budget calls for.

Us: What might happen after that?

Answer: Some of the luxuries we are used to may go away.

Us: What might happen after that?

Answer: We might have to dip into our savings to stay afloat even after cutting back on luxuries.

Us: What might happen after that?

Answer: We may have to alter our lifestyle, including getting rid of one of the cars.

Us: What might happen after that?

Answer: We might have to end up selling our home to downsize because we could no longer afford the mortgage and upkeep.

Us: What might happen after that?

Answer: We would always have a place a live, just not a nice as we have now. Or I could always find employment again.

This was the worst possible scenario for us: selling our home and having to downsize. Once we decided we could live with that, we pulled the trigger and I resigned.

I wish I could tell you that everything worked out like we planned but, no, it did not. We spent way more of our savings staying afloat while I transitioned into being a full-time entrepreneur than we ever thought we would. We never got to the point to selling of our home, but we did have to give up two vacations a year and cut back to one. We ate out a lot less often. We scaled back on our gift giving. We cut many things out of the budget and still were digging into the savings regularly.

My husband has a wonderful way of looking at things. There was a very popular expression several years ago, *"Don't sweat the small stuff."* Whenever I would be stressing over something, my husband would say this to me.

One day, when he let this fall out of his mouth, I turned to him and said, "Well what is the big stuff?"

He calmly looked at me and said, *"*Dying and not knowing the Lord.*"* Since that day, I have learned to stress less!

> *"You must learn to let go. Release the stress. You were never in control anyway." Steve Maraboli*

Going back to Option B: Examine what fear may be holding you back. Ask yourself: Is this fear worth me not going forward? If you really want to try whatever it is you are contemplating, then you need to stare down your fear and move forward although the fear is there. This will take some courage.

Most people think that courage is the absence of fear. Not true. People who have courage feel the fear and do it anyway. That is because they really, really, really want the outcome and are willing to risk being in harm's way to get it.

Not everyone is a risk-taker. People say to me all the time, "I wish I had my own business. I want to be my own boss." After asking them a few questions, I know that they only like the fantasy they have created in their head about their own business. They really are not cut out to be an entrepreneur. They are much more comfortable with being in a support role in an employment situation.

Look at what you wrote for each goal as to why you have not done this yet. Can you identify the root cause as being fear? As we discussed earlier, people's fears fall into very predictable categories:

- Fear of failure
- Fear of being inadequate
- Fear of ridicule
- Fear of going against the grain
- Fear of the unknown
- Fear of change
- Fear of rejection
- Fear of success
- Fear of being embarrassed

- Fear of not being supported
- Fear of losing it all
- Fear of being vulnerable
- Fear of not making enough money
- Fear of missing out on something

Let's look at some scenarios. Let's say you wrote, "I want to finish my degree, but I do not have the money to pay for school."

Ask yourself, "What are the ways I can get the money for school?"
- I can cut back on my living expenses and start to save for the tuition.
  Fear: I might miss out on some fun experiences if I do this.
- Get a student loan.
  Fear: I don't want to be in debt.
- I can borrow from my 401(k).
  Fear: I might not have enough money when I retire.
- I can search to see if I qualify for any grants that I do not have to pay back.
  Fear: I don't want to waste my time.
- I can look for new employment to find an employer that helps me pay for school.
  Fear: Fear of the unknown.

Do you see how many of our decisions not to move forward can be based in fear?

> *"Do one thing every day that scares you."*
> *Eleanor Roosevelt*

Time to Put Fear in its Place!

It's time that you put fear in its right place! In addition to the strategy already given where you look at the worst-case scenario and decide whether you could live with that, here are additional techniques that you should master.

Before we examine them, let's say that there are some things that you fear that have nothing to do with achieving your goals in life. You may have a fear of riding roller coasters. If breaking the Guinness world record for number of roller coasters ridden is not your goal, you are just fine being afraid of them. Or you may have a fear of flying. Unless you really want to be a flight attendant, your life can be pretty amazing avoiding planes forever. Famous stars who will not get on an airplane include Whoopi Goldberg, Sandra Bullock, and Aretha Franklin. And I think we would all agree that they are doing just fine.

So here are some tips on conquering your fears.

- Have a manifesto where you renounce fear. The poem that I wrote serves as my reminder to never let fear hold me back. Write your own fear manifesto or you can use the one below.

    Today and every day, I release fear in my life.
    God has not given me a spirit of fear, but of power, love, and a sound mind.
    God says, "Fear not." I chose to believe God.
    I live my life knowing that God has plans for me, plans to prosper me and not to harm, plans to give me a hope and a future.
    God says if I delight myself in Him, he will give me the desires of my heart.
    The desires that I have come from God.
    I will trust in the Lord with all my heart and know that God is with me every step of the way.
    When I see the word fear, when I hear the word fear, if I ever feel fear, I will remind myself that I have given it a new meaning.

    Fully Expecting Amazing Results

- Value taking risks over security. People need to feel safe. Where you are in your life right now is the known and it is predictable; therefore, it has a certain amount of security. You must be willing to get excited about the opportunities and experiences that taking risks can bring rather than holding on to something that you feel is secure.

> *"Inaction breeds doubt and fear. Action breeds confidence and courage. If you want to conquer fear, do not sit home and think about it. Go out and get busy."* Dale Carnegie

- Become very discerning of the difference between fear and foolishness. If you got a hot stock tip from Harry, who has a cousin-in-law whose ex-wife's fiancée works on Wall Street, and you want to cash out your savings to buy this stock, and you are feeling fearful that you could lose all your money, that is good fear. The stock market on any given day is a gamble. Learn to make good decisions and not foolish ones. A good decision-making technique is to take a sheet a paper and draw a line down the middle. On one side write out all the pros of moving forward and on the other side write out all the cons. Whichever list is larger can help you make a final decision.

- When you feel fear, immediately acknowledge it, and then examine why. Become really good at getting to the root of what you are feeling. Self-examination helps you understand yourself better. In gaining understanding, you are better equipped to deal with the situation if it arises again.

- Lean into your fear and do it anyway. You can start with baby steps and before you know it you will be sprinting!

> *You can, you should, and if you're brave enough to start, you will." Stephen King,*

- Adopt a mindset of abundance. The earth is the Lord's and the fullness thereof! If you think scarcity, you will constantly be afraid of loss. Remember, at the root of all fear is a fear of loss.

- Remember your past victories. Have a place in your home where you can display awards, thank you notes, and other achievements. When you are feeling a bit reluctant about moving in a direction that you want to take, your past successes can make you remember how awesome you really are. This is the only time that it is O.K. to dwell on your past. Do not use this to say, *"I have had enough success. I'll just stay where I am."* Go after your goal!

- Release the idea of embarrassment if something does not work out. Look at it as a learning experience. There is no failure, only feedback. Tell yourself at the beginning of any goal: *"I have full faith and confidence that this is going to work out. That is why I am doing it. Should things turn out differently than I expected, I can't wait to see what I am going to learn."*

> *"If you have a dream, don't just sit there. Gather courage to believe that you can succeed and leave no stone unturned to make it a reality."* Roopleen

- Let people go. Right now, I want you to say this: "What you think of me is none of my business." So many of our fears are rooted in what others might say. Release this. They are going to talk about you anyway.

- Dwell on positive thoughts Spend your time creating in vivid detail what your life will look like when you achieve your goal. Get excited about it so this will serve as the fuel to move you forward. Philippians 4:8 tells us, "Whatever things are true, whatever things are noble, whatever things are just, whatever things are pure, whatever things are lovely, "whatever things are of good report, if there is any virtue and if there is anything praiseworthy— meditate on these things." (NKJV)

> "When you concentrate your energy purposely on the future possibility that you aspire to realize, your energy is passed on to it and makes it attracted to you with a force stronger than the one you directed towards it."
> Stephen Richards

Chapter Five

Aligning Your Goals With the True You

Have you ever taken a personality test? There are many different versions available. Some are very complicated and come up with esoteric names that are often difficult to remember. I have taken the Meyer-Briggs personality test on more than one occasion, and I still can't recall what my personality type is!

The Bible says that you are *"fearfully and wonderfully made."* Your personality type was set at birth. This is a gift from God. For those of us who have raised two or more children you know this to be true. They come from the womb just as different as day is from night!

As I already stated, some of us spend so much of our lives trying to be like someone else. We compare ourselves to others to see how we are measuring up. This is a very harmful practice. It is O.K. to have role models and people we look up to and admire. Aspiring to be like them is O.K. too if it is aligned with who you are at the core.

In this section, you are going to take two types of tests: A spiritual gifts test and a personality test. This will give you a well-rounded view of who you really are.

Spiritual Gifts

This information on Spiritual Gifts is taken from LifeWay Christian Resources (http://www.lifeway.com/lwc/files/lwcf_pdf_discover_your_spiritual_gifts.pdf)

A spiritual gift is a special attribute given by the Holy Spirit to every member of the Body of Christ for use within the context of the church. The gifts are referenced in Romans 12:6-8; 1 Corinthians 12:8-10, 28-30; Ephesians 4:11; and 1 Peter 4:9-11. The gifts are as follows:

• Leadership—Leadership aids the body by leading and directing members to accomplish the goals and purposes of the church. Leadership motivates people to work together in unity toward common goals (Rom. 12:8).

• Administration—Persons with the gift of administration lead the body by steering others to remain on task. Administration enables the body to organize according to God-given purposes and long-term goals (1 Cor. 12:28).

• Teaching—Teaching is instructing members in the truths and doctrines of God's Word for the purposes of building up, unifying, and maturing the body (1 Cor. 12:28; Rom. 12:7; Eph. 4:11).

• Knowledge—The gift of knowledge manifests itself in teaching and training in discipleship. It is the God-given ability to learn, know, and explain the precious truths of God's Word. A word of knowledge is a Spirit-revealed truth (1 Cor. 12:28).

• Wisdom—Wisdom is the gift that discerns the work of the Holy Spirit in the body and applies His teachings and actions to the needs of the body (1 Cor. 12:28).

• Prophecy—The gift of prophecy is proclaiming the Word of God boldly. This builds up the body and leads to conviction of sin. Prophecy manifests itself in preaching and teaching (1 Cor. 12:10; Rom. 12:6).

• Discernment—Discernment aids the body by recognizing the true intentions of those within or related to the body. Discernment tests the message and actions of others for the protection and well-being of the body (1 Cor. 12:10).

• Exhortation—Possessors of this gift encourage members to be involved in and get enthusiastic about the work of the Lord. Members with this gift are good counselors and motivate others to service. Exhortation exhibits itself in preaching, teaching, and ministry (Rom. 12:8).

• Shepherding—The gift of shepherding is manifested in persons who look out for the spiritual welfare of others. Although pastors, like shepherds, do care for members of the church, this gift is not limited to a pastor or staff member (Eph. 4:11).

• Faith—Faith trusts God to work beyond the human capabilities of the people. Believers with this gift encourage others to trust in God in the face of apparently insurmountable odds (1 Cor. 12:9).

• Evangelism—God gifts his church with evangelists to lead others to Christ effectively and enthusiastically. This gift builds up the body by adding new members to its fellowship (Eph. 4:11).

• Apostleship—The church sends apostles from the body to plant churches or to be missionaries. Apostles motivate the body to look beyond its walls in order to carry out the Great Commission (1 Cor. 12:28; Eph. 4:11).

• Service/Helps—Those with the gift of service/help recognize practical needs in the body and joyfully give assistance to meeting those needs. Christians with this gift do not mind working behind the scenes (1 Cor. 12:28; Rom. 12:7).

• Mercy—Cheerful acts of compassion characterize those with the gift of mercy. Persons with this gift aid the body by empathizing with hurting members. They keep the body healthy and unified by keeping others aware of the needs within the church (Rom. 12:8).

• Giving—Members with the gift of giving give freely and joyfully to the work and mission of the body. Cheerfulness and liberality are characteristics of individuals with this gift (Rom. 12:8).

Assignment Seven

It is time for you to determine your spiritual gifts. For the spiritual gifts test, you have two options. The first is a downloadable PDF form that you can print out and keep a copy of. Many people like this better than the online version because they have a hard copy of their answers and do not need to be in front of a computer to take the test.

Copy and paste this link into your browser:
http://www.lifeway.com/lwc/files/lwcf_pdf_discover_your_spiritual_gifts.pdf

The other is an online version that will take you approximately 10 minutes. Go to www.spiritualgifttest.com. You do not need to register or give any personal information to take the test.

Once you have completed the test, write what your top three spiritual gifts are in the space below.

_____
_____
_____
_____

Assignment Eight

Let's move on to the personality test. You also have two options.

This first one, called Psychogeometrics, is my favorite because you only must answer one question. It is surprisingly accurate and it not only gives you your personality type, but also tells you your strengths, weaknesses, and what professions best suit you. As mentioned earlier, I have taken other tests and could never quite remember my personality type. Not only did I always remember my personality type because of this test, but I can easily spot the personalities of others and remember what qualities are associated with their personality type.

The test is in a PDF file at:
http://willamette.edu/offices/careers/pdf/Psychogeometrics%20Willamette%202010.pdf

The second personality test is a test you take online. You can just take the Psychogeometrics test, just take the one below, or take both. It is totally up to you.

http://www.16personalities.com/free-personality-test

In the space below write out in detail what the tests reveal about you. Explore if this is the way you see yourself. If you feel the test did not accurately reflect you, then craft your own description of who you believe you are.

Assignment Nine

My personality type is:

_____
_____
_____
_____
_____

The strengths of my personality type are:
_____
_____
_____
_____

Some of the weaknesses of my personality type are:
_____
_____
_____
_____
_____
_____
_____

Professions that I am best suited for are:
_____
_____
_____
_____
_____
_____
_____
_____
_____
_____

My spiritual gifts are:

_____
_____
_____
_____
_____
_____

Assignment Ten

It is now time to determine what goals you are ready to commit to. Consider:
- The goals that you put through the system using the worst-case scenario
- Your personality
- Your spiritual gifts
- What you would do if you could not fail
- What you would do for free
- How you would live your life if money were no object
- What it is that you do that people compliment you on
- Everything you have read in this book
- Everything you have felt in the book

I am committing to the following goals:

> "Setting goals is the first step in turning the invisible into the visible." Tony Robbins

Chapter Six
What Motivates You?

Now that you have your goal(s) clear, let's look at what motivates you to achieve. There are both external factors and internal factors that motivate us.

External factors are those that you have no control over. This could be a contest that your company is sponsoring and the reward is a free trip to some exotic island. You had no control over what the company offered or what the parameters were for achieving the prize.

Internal factors are more tied to your personality type and what you derive satisfaction from. Knowing what motivates you will help you guide your action plan that you are soon going to create to achieve your goal. You must be motivated from within to achieve your goal. If you are doing it for someone else, you will never achieve your goal. To clarify, you may be motivated to finish college so you can get a better-paying job to provide a certain standard of living for your family. While your family benefits from this, you are doing this for the satisfaction that it will bring you.

Assignment Eleven

Below are 8 factors that you are going to rate yourself on. For each factor give it a score of 1 to 5, 1 being not that important to you and 5 being of high importance. Do not judge yourself because of how you rate each one. Just be honest, as this will help you understand yourself better.

1. I want to be a high achiever and be recognized for my accomplishments.

   1   2   3   4   5

2. I like having nice things and the luxurious feel of nice things in my space.

   1   2   3   4   5

3. I like being a part of a group of people with common goals and interests like clubs, sororities, and fraternities.

   1   2   3   4   5

4. I like being independent and working on my own.

   1   2   3   4   5

5. I like to create. I don't like the status quo and like coming up with new ideas.

   1   2   3   4   5

6. I like having a title and being socially recognized.

   1   2   3   4   5

7. I like having power over others and influencing people and events.

   1   2   3   4   5

8. I like playing it safe. Risk bothers me.

   1   2   3   4   5

9. I like to serve others and make a difference.

   1   2   3   4   5

Remember, this is a judgment-free zone. Which ones did you rank a 5? If you ranked more than one a 5, look at them and rank them in order of 1, 2, 3, etc. This is only for the ones you have ranked 5.

My top three motivators are:

_____
_____
_____
_____

Now that you know what motivates you, you will create that scenario as you focus on achieving your dream. This will make sense when we to get the section on affirmations.

> *"People often say that motivation doesn't last. Well, neither does bathing - that's why we recommend it daily." Zig Ziglar*

Chapter Seven
Your Action Plan

Now that you have identified your goal(s) and know what some of your internal motivators are, the next step is to create in detail an action plan that will get and keep you motivated to achieve your goal. If you have more than one goal that you would like to work on simultaneously, just re-create this section as many times as you need to.

The system we will use to help you establish and achieve your goal is called the SMART system. I have tweaked this a little and identified SMART goals as being specific, measurable, action plan, realistic, and time-bound.

Look at the goal(s) that you want to achieve. Are they specific? A goal that says, "I will do better with my finances" is not specific. A goal that says, "I will establish and adhere to a budget" is specific. Now you may start with a general goal that you want to improve your finances, but each step toward that goal must be specific.

Not only does your goal have to be specific, it has to be measurable. A measurable goal is one that anyone can look at and evaluate whether you did or did not achieve what you set out to do. When you write your goal, leave out the words "I want." Write your goal using the words "I will." For example, "I will write and publish a book on interior design."

The goal must have an action plan. An action plan is exactly what you will do to achieve your goal. This is the missing piece to most goal setting. You must have the very specific steps that you will take each day, each week, each month in order to achieve your goal.

Once you have written out the specific steps, you have to ask yourself if it is realistic. Both your goal and the steps that you wrote to achieve it must pass the test. For example, if you start with a goal that you want to be a ballerina and perform with the American Ballet Theatre, and you are now over 30, this goal is not realistic. You must be no older than 22 to audition.

Each goal that you write must have a time for when it will be achieved. A goal without a deadline is just a dream. A deadline commits you to the goal and sets a fire under you so you can keep moving forward.

Assignment Twelve

My goal is

_____
_____
_____

_____

_____

_____

Copy your goal on a sheet of paper and paste it in places where you will see it every day. Put it in your wallet, on your dashboard, on your desk at work ... put it everywhere! Seeing your goal in writing daily will help you focus on it.

Next, write the date when you will accomplish your goal. Having a timeframe to achieve your goal is imperative. Don't feel like if you set a date by which to achieve it this will box you in. This is flexible and timelines can be adjusted. But you must have a timeframe.

I will accomplish this by:

_____

Now, identify the actual actions that you need to take to reach your goal. This is where most goal setting goes awry. People are good at stating what they want. They can also tell you when they want it. But creating an action plan and sticking with it ... that is where the rubber meets the road and most people go off the road! So get very clear on each action that you must take. Each action must have an associated deadline. If you need to gain more information to go about achieving your goal, set the deadlines for when that will happen. This action plan must be completed with all the steps it will take you to reach your goal. It is perfectly fine to break your goal into smaller goals, with each smaller goal leading to the big goal.

Let me share with you an example of an action plan that I created. I wanted to reach a certain rank in a network marketing company that I was affiliated with. There were 30-day, 90-day, and 180-day bonuses that were associated with rank advancements. When I signed my name on the dotted line, I knew what I wanted to achieve and when I wanted to achieve it. This is what my goal statement looked like.

Goal statement: I will be a Diamond Executive by _____(I wrote in a date).

To break this goal down, I listed dates when I would achieve the other two ranks.

I will be a Manager by

_____

I will be a Director by

_____

My action plan

I will speak with 25 people a week about my business. To do this, I will speak with 6 people a day, Monday-Thursday, with Friday and Saturday available in the event I need to make up.

These contacts will come from my cell phone, my email, and friends that I have on Facebook.

I will have a one-on-one conversation, a personal text, or a personal message on FB.

I will follow up with everyone that I speak to within 48 hours or at the time they say is convenient.

I will host 2 in-home parties per month.

I will attend two networking events per week to make new contacts.

I will post in 25 Facebook groups per day.

I will keep in touch with everyone I have spoken to about my business with a bi-monthly healthy tip news blast.

Notice how these action steps are very specific. I can look back and say either I did or I didn't do the things I said I would do. The advantage of having the steps very specific and measurable is that if I am not getting the results that I want, I know what activity I need to increase.

Now it is your turn. Write out exactly what you plan to do and when you plan on doing it.

My action plan:
_____
_____
_____
_____
_____
_____
_____
_____
_____
_____
_____
_____
_____
_____
_____
_____
_____
_____
_____
_____

Set your eyes on your goal and never, never, look back. You cannot give up at the first sign of challenges. Will everything go smoothly? Of course not! Will there be obstacles that you must overcome? Guarantee it! But obstacles are what you see when you take your eyes off the goal.

Might you stumble, fail, and have to re-group? Yep! Failure is only proof that that you are trying! And look at so-called failures with another mindset: failure is only feedback.

People who achieve great things fail more than anyone else. They fell down and had to get back up. Many celebrities had major failures before they became successful.

- Oprah Winfrey was publicly fired from her first television anchor job in Baltimore, Maryland, because she became too emotionally invested in her stories.
- R.H. Macy, the founder of Macy's, had several failed retail ventures before he opened his first Macy's store.
- Harrison Ford, the star of the *Indiana Jones* movie series, was told by a director after his first role in a movie that he would never make it in the movies.
- Dr. Seuss had his first book rejected by 27 publishing companies.

- Michael Jordan was cut from his high school basketball team.
- Lady Gaga was dropped by her first record label after only 3 months.
- Henry Ford, the founder of the Ford Motor Company, had ruined his reputation after having several failed automobile businesses.

Can you guess who this person is?

In one year, he lost his job and lost his bid for state legislature. The next year his business failed. Two years later, his bride-to-be died before they were married. The next year he had a nervous breakdown. Two years later he ran for speaker in the state legislature and was defeated. Five years later he ran for congress and lost. Two years later he was elected to congress, but he lost when he attempted to run two years after that. Six years later he lost the election for U.S. senate. Two years later he lost the nomination for Vice President of the U.S. Two years later he was defeated for U.S. senate. And two years after that, he became the 16th President of the United States.

Allow me to introduce you to Abraham Lincoln. Talk about tenacity!

Successful people are not smarter than others. They are not prettier, nor have better backgrounds. They were simply not defeated by setbacks. They continued chasing after their dreams. They kept on trying long enough to make it.

Unsuccessful people give up early. They see their mistakes as signs of their inadequacy.

To achieve your dream, you are going to have to step out of your comfort zone. You are going to have to decide to be uncomfortable for a while. You may think your comfort zone is safe, but it is really a prison.

Winners don't win all the time. They sometimes lose. It is what you do at that point that makes a difference.

Assignment Thirteen

Write out what your life will look when you succeed. Write this out in clear detail and let your imagination run free. Describe what an average day would like for you. Tell the places you will travel to for business or pleasure. How will your success impact the quality time you spend with your family and friends? What charitable causes will you be involved in as a result? Based on what your internal motivators are, how do you see yourself being rewarded? Is it stepping on stage to receive an award? Is it being invited to join a select group? Is it buying a boat or Porsche? Write out everything!

When I Achieve My Goal This is What My Life Will Look Like

_____
_____
_____
_____
_____
_____
_____
_____
_____
_____
_____
_____
_____
_____
_____
_____
_____
_____
_____
_____

Once you have this completed, read it aloud to yourself every day. Every day. Several times a day. Every day until you have achieved the goal. You can modify it or add more details to it. But keep a clear mental picture of the life you desire so it will inspire you daily.

Chapter Eight
Affirmations

Affirmations are positive statements that you speak aloud frequently that describe what you want. They are usually no more than 10 to 15 words in length.

Affirmations affect both the conscious and subconscious mind. When you repeat affirmations often, they will inevitably influence your behavior and cause you to take certain actions. And the actions you take are what will ultimately cause you to achieve your goal. If you have ever used affirmations, you know that they can be a powerful motivator. They are like the oil that keeps the fire burning to keep your dream alive.

It is believed that the best time to repeat affirmations is upon awakening every morning. Supposedly, this is when the subconscious mind is most open to receiving the information. It may be that the first minutes of your waking day are set aside for your devotional time so you are not comfortable with doing affirmations first. This is totally understandable. I would encourage you to just include them as part of your morning routine. They will help you get your day started in the right direction, and they beat a cup of coffee for a morning boost!

There are different schools of thought on how affirmations should be couched. For example, if your goal is to lose weight and you know the ideal weight that you want to achieve, your affirmation statement could be one of the following:

- I weigh 150 pounds (although you currently weigh a lot more)
- I am in the process of reaching my ideal weight of 150 pounds

Some believe that if you say something about yourself that is not true, then the subconscious mind rebels against accepting it. So the first statement would not be effective. However, telling yourself what you are in the process of doing is a truer statement and therefore more acceptable to your subconscious. I have known people to use both; choose whichever you are most comfortable with.

Assignment Fourteen

You will now write your own affirmations to align with exactly what you want to achieve. Include in your affirmations some of your internal motivators. All affirmations are written in the positive, not in the negative. When you write your affirmations, say what you want, not what you don't want.

- Correct: I earn money very easily

- Incorrect: I no longer want to struggle earning money
- Correct: My body is healthy and full and energy
- Incorrect: I will stop feeling sluggish and exercise more.

I like to keep my affirmations on 3x 5 cards that I have cut in half. They can fit very neatly into my purse and I carry them with me wherever I go. Sometimes, I just repeat them aloud from memory. I also say them when I am driving in my car, especially when I am stuck in traffic!

When you say your affirmations aloud, just don't read them as if you were reading a sentence. You must infuse them enthusiasm, energy, and belief. Be emphatic when you state them. Add your emotions into them. Stomp your feet, clap your hands, bang on the table! Laugh, be joyous, and be determined! These emotions coupled with the statement help to accelerate your results.

All of this may feel a little unnatural at first. You may even have doubts that you will achieve what you are affirming. It is not only what you say out of your mouth that has power, it is what you whisper to yourself. So when your mind talks back to you and says something negative, get sassy and talk back!

Just stick with it and don't give up. Any new habit that you want to acquire requires repetition. Before long, it will become a natural part of who you are. You will get very comfortable saying these positive things about yourself.

Here are just a few affirmations to give you an idea of what you can write.

- I love the person I am becoming
- I am full of energy and love
- I focus daily on the habits that lead to success
- I am friendly to everyone that I meet
- I am in the process of becoming an international speaker
- I am a well-known author
- My blog is read by thousands of people
- I am patient with my children
- I am in the process of opening my business
- My health is improving every day
- I eat foods that build my body up
- I travel the world
- I vacation 3 months a year

- I am grateful for all God has allowed in my life
- I am building my income to $20,000 a month

Some of my favorite affirmations involve scripture. Hebrews 4:12a tells us, *"For the word of God is quick and powerful."* (NKJV) Why not use the power of God's word to put your life on an exciting course?

I am in habit of personalizing what the word of God says. For example, Jeremiah 29:11: *"For I know the plans I have for you," declares the Lord," plans to prosper you and not to harm, plans to give you a hope and a future."* (NIV) I have re-stated this to say, *"For I know the plans God has for me. Plans to prosper me and not to harm me. Plans to give me a hope and a future."* Now you could argue here that I since I personalized it is no longer scripture. Understandable. Do what makes you comfortable.

Some other scripture affirmations that I like to use are listed below from the New King James translation.

Philippians 4:13: *"I can do all things through Christ who strengthens me."*

Philippians 4:19: *"My God shall apply of all of my needs according to his riches in glory by Christ Jesus."*

Ephesians 3:20: *"My God is able to exceedingly, abundantly, above all I could ask or think."*

Matthew 19:26: "*With God all things are possible.*"

John 10:10: "*Jesus came that I would have life, and have it more abundantly.*"

Psalm 139:14: "*I am fearfully and wonderfully made.*"

Deuteronomy 28:13: "*I am the head and not the tail.*"

One of my favorite scripture affirmations that I rewrote and personalized is Proverbs 31, 10-31. Oh yes I did! Why not set my goals on being a woman that scripture admires? Here is the New King James version of it:

10 Who can find a virtuous wife? For her worth is far above rubies.
11 The heart of her husband safely trusts her; so he will have no lack of gain.
12 She does him good and not evil all the days of her life.
13 She seeks wool and flax, and willingly works with her hands.
14 She is like the merchant ships, she brings her food from afar.
15 She also rises while it is yet night, and provides food for her household, and a portion for her maidservants.
16 She considers a field and buys it; from her profits she plants a vineyard.
17 She girds herself with strength, and strengthens her arms.

¹⁸ She perceives that her merchandise is good, and her lamp does not go out by night.

¹⁹ She stretches out her hands to the distaff, and her hand holds the spindle.

²⁰ She extends her hand to the poor, yes, she reaches out her hands to the needy.

²¹ She is not afraid of snow for her household, for all her household is clothed with scarlet.

²² She makes tapestry for herself; her clothing is fine linen and purple.

²³ Her husband is known in the gates, when he sits among the elders of the land.

²⁴ She makes linen garments and sells them, and supplies sashes for the merchants.

²⁵ Strength and honor are her clothing; she shall rejoice in time to come.

⁶ She opens her mouth with wisdom, and on her tongue is the law of kindness.

²⁷ She watches over the ways of her household, and does not eat the bread of idleness.

²⁸ Her children rise up and call her blessed; her husband also, and he praises her.

²⁹ "Many daughters have done well, but you excel them all."

³⁰ Charm is deceitful and beauty is passing, but a woman who fears the Lord, she shall be praised.

³¹ Give her of the fruit of her hands, and let her own works praise her in the gates.

This is my personalized version of Proverbs 31. I have it printed and it is hanging in my office. And if after you read it you think I had some nerve – you're right! I kind of like me!

I am a virtuous wife. My worth is far more than rubies.

My husband is full of confidence is me and he lacks nothing of value.

I bring him good and not harm all of the days of his life.

I select choice words and work them into literary masterpieces.

I am like the merchant ships, bringing my food from afar.

I get up while it is still night and provide food for my family and portions for others.

I consider my business and join it; out of my earnings I re-invest.

I set about my work vigorously; my arms are strong for my tasks.

I see that my efforts are profitable and my lamp does not go out at night.

My laptop is on my lap and I extend my hands to the keyboard.

I open my arms to the poor and extend my hands to the needy.

When it snows, I have no fear for my household, for all of them are clothed in warm clothing.

I purchase coverings for my bed and I am clothed in fine garments.

My husband is respected among friends and family and he takes his seat at the head of the table.

I create books and sell them, which provides knowledge to others.

I am clothed in strength and dignity and can laugh at the days to come.

I speak with wisdom, and faithful instruction is on my tongue.

I watch over the affairs of my household and do not eat the bread of idleness.

My children have arisen and call me blessed, my husband also praises me.

Many women do noble things, but I surpass them all.

Charm is deceptive, and beauty is fleeting, but I fear the Lord and I am to be praised.

Honor me for all that my hands have done, and let my works bring me praise in the community.

Chapter Nine

Vision Boards

Many successful people use visualization to help them achieve their goals. A vision board is a tangible visualization. It is a visual reminder of your goals and the lifestyle you will enjoy once you achieve your goals.

Jack Canfield, well-known author and success coach, believes that creating a vision board is one of the most powerful visualization tools available. He states, *"Your brain will work tirelessly to achieve the statements you give your subconscious mind. And when those statements are affirmation and images of your goals, you are destined to achieve them!"* (http://jackcanfield.com/how-to-create-an-empowering-vision-borad/#sthas.vUC23OPE.dpuf)

A vision board is normally a collection of pictures and phrases. You may have pictures of places you have visited or would like to visit, items you will buy, people you will spend time with, the title of an article written about you, the amount of a future check, a future promotion, etc. You can also include words that evoke emotion for you, such as some of your affirmations or words like powerful, strong, confident, motivated, blessed, etc.

The pictures you use can come from just about anywhere. Use your personal photos, magazine photos, or download photos or scenes from the internet.

A vision board can help you accomplish just about any goal. When I work with clients who want to lose weight, I encourage them to put their goal weight on the board and the dress/pant size that they want to be. They also put pictures of outfits that they desire to buy in the new size or outfits that they own that they are determined to be able to wear again. They post pictures of healthy food, the gym, and other reminders of things they will do to achieve their goal. They also post compliments that they know they will receive once they reach their goal.

You can use a variety of materials to make a vision board. I have used cork bulletin boards, the tri-fold stand-up boards that most children use for science projects, and poster board. My most recent board is a tri-fold stand-up that I keep in my office. My office is on the first floor of my home and is rather cozy with a sofa and T.V. Because it flows right off the living room, it is normal that family and friends end up in my office. When I know that guests are coming, I put the board away.

Now why would I do that? Because many people who I love and whose company I enjoy can't handle my vision for my life. Hence, I don't share my goals and dreams with everybody. In fact, I share them with very few people. This is something that you will undoubtedly learn as you work toward your goals. Not everyone is going to cheer you on, so you will want to protect dreams from the naysayers.

The vision board should take you to a happy place when you see it. The board should make you feel as if you were already living your dream and your goal has been accomplished. It should not serve as pressure for you to accomplish whatever you have decided to accomplish. If this is what you feel when you see it, then you need to reconsider what you have put on your board.

I look at my vision board daily and read everything on it. I do not read it – I proclaim it! I feel so energized after I have a spent a few minutes with my future!

Here are some of the items on my current vision board.

- My life mission statement is at the center, which reads, *"My mission is to love the Lord my God with all my heart, mind, and soul as evidenced by a reputation of integrity and a life of service to others and to impact lives by sharing truth."*

- A picture of my grandson. He is part of my happy place. His picture reminds me to do my best and take good care of myself. I want to be on the planet as long as possible and in good health to see him grow up.
- Pictures of me and my husband vacationing.
- Other pictures of family, both immediate and extended, reminding me that they are the most important ones to spend time with.
- A picture of me driving a pontoon boat. This is the one toy I still want to own.
- A picture of me with school children in Kapsabet, Kenya. I was a short-term missionary in Kapsabet and I want to do more missionary trips. Also, the picture clarifies my goal of feeding hungry children around the world.
- A picture of Egypt, Paris, and the Panama Canal. These are places I have yet to visit but desire to do so.
- A picture of my home and the date it will be paid off.
- Several "headlines" of news articles detailing the accomplishments of our company, including the millions of women WEEE have helped and the millions of meals WEEE have donated to feed hungry children.

As you create your vision board, make sure it inspires you and you enjoy looking at it. Make sure there is a clear connection on the board to the goal you are trying to achieve. For example, if you goal is to get healthy, then having a date when your mortgage is paid off, although that would probably make you smile, is not relevant to what you are trying to achieve.

Now go create your vision!

110

Chapter Ten

Get Around The Right People

One thing that decelerates your progress faster than anything I know is being around the wrong people. It has been said that a person can tell where you are heading in life by the people you surround yourself with. Once you get clarity on what you want, you must begin to associate with people of like minds that can help you on your journey.

And let me give you a warning: If you get clarity on something you want to go for and it seems like a stretch for you, be careful of the people who may be closest to you who try to discourage you from moving forward.

There are reasons why people who say they love you don't want you to move forward from where you are right now. One, they want to keep you safe. Whenever a person attempts anything new, there is always the risk that it will not work out. If it doesn't work out, they assume you will be hurt and broken. They see their actions as loving and kind and only wanting the best for you.

The second reason is that they do not want to see you doing new things because they do not know what the new you will look like or how it will behave. They are comfortable with you just the way you are and that is the you they like. A new you is a scary proposition. They don't want to lose the person they know.

A third reason is that it might cause them to have to look at their own life and see where improvement can be made. Self-examination is challenging and, unless a person is ready to grow, your growth will make them uncomfortable.

The fourth reason is that they simply do not want to see you succeed and do better than them. People who are already successful usually encourage others to be successful too. People who are not successful will say and do whatever it takes to keep you down.

Some of my favorite quotes on choosing to hang around the right people are as follows.

- *"Associate yourself with people of good quality, for it is better to be alone than in bad company."* Booker T. Washington

- *"You become like the 5 people you spend the most time with. Choose carefully."* Unknown

- *"Surround yourself with only people who are going to lift you higher."* Oprah Winfrey

- *"To be of good quality, you have to excuse yourself from the presence of shallow and callow minded individuals."* Michael Bassey

- *"Make a conscious effort to surround yourself with positive, nourishing, and uplifting people – people who believe in you, encourage you to go after your dreams, and applaud your victories."* Jack Canfield.

- *"Keep away from people who belittle your ambition."* Mark Twain

- *"Always surround yourself with people who are better than you. If you're hanging around bad people, they're going to start bringing you down. But if you surround yourself with good people, they're going to be pulling you up."* Donny Osmond

The Bible has a lot to say about hanging around the wrong people. All scripture from New King James Bible Translation.

- Proverbs 12:26: *"The righteous choose their friends carefully, but the way of the wicked leads them astray."*

- Proverbs 13:20: *"Walk with the wise and become wise; associate with fools and get in trouble."*

- 1 Corinthians 15:33: *"Do not be misled: Bad company corrupts good character."*

- Psalm 1:1: *"How blessed is the man who does not walk in the counsel of the wicked, nor stand in the path of sinners, nor sit in the seat of scoffers."*

- Proverbs 22:24-25: *"Do not be a friend of one who has a bad temper, and never keep company with a hothead, or you will learn his ways and set a trap for yourself."*

- 2 Corinthians 6:14: *"Do not be bound together with unbelievers; for what partnership have righteousness and lawlessness, or what fellowship has light with darkness?"*

If you assess who your current friends and find you need an upgrade, don't be discouraged. In this electronic age that we live in, it is easy to connect with new groups of people. Now these may or may not become your friends and they may only make it to the level of acquaintance, but they can still be a valuable source of support. And you don't necessarily lose your old friends. You may need to spend less time with them as you invest in growing yourself into the awesome man or woman of God that you desire to be.

Meetup.com is a great way to meet new people in your area who can encourage you in pursuing your goals.

Women Enlightened & Economically Empowered offers Mastermind groups that you can join. These are both virtual and live group meetings. You can find out more about these groups at www.womeneee.com

You can enroll in a class in your local community college that helps you grow in the area you need to grow in to reach your goals.

Volunteering in your area of interest is also a good way to meet new people in your area of interest.

Whatever method you employ, make the commitment to surround yourself with positive people who can lift you up and encourage you on your journey to success.

Chapter 11

Time To Accelerate!!!

DO THE WORK!

You now have the knowledge of some powerful strategies that you can use to accelerate to achieve any goal you want to achieve. Get out of the way, eliminate excuses, and create your best life. It is now time to DO THE WORK!

If all you do is read this book and do not apply it, then you have just wasted your time. Wisdom is knowledge applied, not knowledge learned. The victory comes in doing, not in knowing.

Just a few words of advice as you set out to achieve your goals.

- Find at least one person who you can share your goals with so they can hold you accountable and cheer you on. Everyone needs at least one fan.
- Don't beat yourself up if you miss doing your affirmations or fall short one week with the steps you were supposed to take for your action plan. A setback is just setup for comeback!
- Surround yourself with positive people who have a dream.

- Consider learning how to do visualizations. This will further accelerate your progress.
- Hire a personal life coach if you feel you need that support. We have some great coaches at WEEE!
- Do plug into Women Enlightened & Economically Empowered, LLC motivational calls. See the website at www.womenee.com for details. They are inspiring.

And in closing: *"Beloved I wish above all things that you prosper and be in health, even as your soul prospers."* 3 John 1:2 (NKJV)

About The Author

Etrulia Reid Troy Lee (Dr. Troy) is a life coach/health coach, holistic educator, author, motivational speaker, and entrepreneur. She is the CEO and founder of Women Enlightened & Economically Empowered, LLC, (WEEE) a company that offers online coaching for women, mentoring, and mastermind groups. WEEE also enables women to earn income through their referral program and social entrepreneurship business model. WEEE donates 20% of their profits to feed hungry children worldwide.

Dr. Troy holds Bachelor and Master's degrees in education and a doctorate in holistic nutrition from Clayton College of Natural Health. She has authored several books including *Phonics is My Way*, a reading series for children, *Eat Yourself Slim and Never Diet Again, Get Your "But" Out of the Way: Your 30-Day Guide to Eliminating Excuses so You Can Create Your Best Life,* and *Principled Success: How I Went From Low Income and Low Self-Esteem to Confidence & Prosperity.*

Her past professional positions include classroom teacher, Education Administrator at Hospital for Sick Children, Educational Consultant, principal for SHABACH! Christian Academy, instructor at the USDA Graduate School, Education Division Superintendent for SHABACH! Ministries, Inc., adjunct professor of nutrition at Global Health College, and independent trainer. She has served as a Sunday school teacher, director of children's church, member of the church board of directors, facilitator for the discipleship series *Master Life,* and short-term missionary to Kenya.

Dr. Troy is a sought-after speaker and is very creative and energetic in her presentations. She has presented engaging seminars for many groups, including White House employees, government employees, church groups, and civic groups. She has been a featured speaker at numerous women conferences and has been a guest on T.V. and radio.

Seminar topics include:

- How to Write a Personal Mission Statement to Achieve Your Destiny
- The Principles and Power of Goal Setting: How to Create an Action Plan to Achieve Your Goals
- Get Fierce! How to Recognize and Release Fears So You Can Soar
- From Excuses to Excellence

- Mission Possible: You Can Do It!
- Conflict Resolution in the Workplace
- Making Forgiveness a Lifestyle: How to Let Go of the Baggage and Be Free
- Eat Yourself Slim and Never Diet Again
- What Every Parent and Should Know About How the Brain Develops
- Nutrition and Learning
- Healthy Lifestyles: Nutrition, Stress Reduction, and Exercise
- Are You Losing Your Mind? How Different Foods Affect the Structure and Function of the Brain
- Is Your Body on Fire? Understanding Inflammation: The Number One Cause of Sickness and Disease

Dr. Troy is a native of Philadelphia, PA. She has resided in the Washington D.C. metro area since 1978 and currently makes her home in Fort Washington, MD, where she lives with husband, Arvid Lee. She has two adult sons, Chay & Michael, one daughter-in-love, Jenene, married to Michael. Michael and Jenene have blessed her with one adorable grandson, Collin Anderson Lee.

To book Dr. Troy for a speaking engagement, keynote, training, MC, or panelist, contact her office at info@womeneee.com

www.ingramcontent.com/pod-product-compliance
Lightning Source LLC
LaVergne TN
LVHW061312060426
835507LV00019B/2117